Read-About® Holidays

Earth Day

By Trudi Strain Trueit

Reading Consultant
Cecilia Minden–Cupp, PhD
Former Director of the Language and Literacy Program
Harvard Graduate School of Education
Cambridge, Massachusetts

Children's Press®
A Division of Scholastic Inc.
New York   Toronto   London   Auckland   Sydney
Mexico City   New Delhi   Hong Kong
Danbury, Connecticut

3 1984 00252 8816

Designer: Herman Adler
Photo Researcher: Caroline Anderson
The photo on the cover shows children planting a tree.

Library of Congress Cataloging-in-Publication Data

Trueit, Trudi Strain.
  Earth Day / by Trudi Strain Trueit.
    p. cm. — (Rookie read-about holidays)
  ISBN 10: 0-531-12455-X (lib. bdg.)   0-531-11836-3 (pbk.)
  ISBN 13: 978-0-531-12455-0 (lib. bdg.)   978-0-531-11836-8 (pbk.)
  1. Earth Day—Juvenile literature. 2. Environmentalism—Juvenile
literature. 3. Environmental protection—Juvenile literature. I. Title.
II. Series.
  GE195.5.T78 2006
  394.262—dc22   2006004433

CHILDREN'S PRESS, and ROOKIE READ-ABOUT®, and associated
logos are trademarks and/or registered trademarks of Scholastic Library
Publishing. SCHOLASTIC and associated logos are trademarks and/or
registered trademarks of Scholastic Inc.
1 2 3 4 5 6 7 8 9 10 R 16 15 14 13 12 11 10 09 08 07

Imagine a city where the air is so dirty it is hard to breathe. Imagine a lake so full of oil that no fish or wildlife can live there.

Some places in the United States were like this fifty years ago. People didn't think as much about the environment (en-VYE-ruhn-muhnt) back then. The environment is the air, land, and water we need to survive.

A polluted lake

Dangerous chemicals being dumped into a river

Factories filled the air with smoke and pollution. Cars let off more gas fumes than they do today.

Companies dumped dangerous materials into rivers. Chemicals (KEM-uh-kuhlz) used by farmers to grow food also damaged the soil.

U.S. senator Gaylord Nelson felt America should be doing more to take care of the planet. He wanted to teach people how to protect Earth's air, soil, water, plants, and animals. This idea is known as conservation (kon-sur-VAY-shuhn).

Senator Gaylord Nelson

April 2007

Sunday	Monday	Tuesday	Wednesday	Thursday	Friday	Saturday
1	2	3	4	5	6	7
8	9	10	11	12	13	14
15	16	17	18	19	20	21
22	23	24	25	26	27	28
29	30					

Senator Nelson wanted
to get more young people
interested in conservation,
so he created Earth Day.
The first Earth Day was
held on April 22, 1970.

Millions of students took part in marches. They gave speeches. They asked world leaders to take action to save the environment.

Children today continue to celebrate Earth Day
with parades.

Electric cars are good for the environment.

Earth Day made a difference. Laws were passed to protect the environment. Carmakers had to build cars that created less pollution. Many harmful chemicals were outlawed.

Cities began to recycle. People turned in used paper, glass, and plastic. These items were later made into new products. Boxes, bags, and packing materials are all things that can be reused.

Kids participating in a recycling project

Planting a tree on Earth Day

Ways to Celebrate

Most nations around the world celebrate Earth Day. Children in Australia pick up litter, or trash, along beaches. People in the United States and Canada plant trees.

Russian students plant vegetable gardens. They learn to grow food without using harmful chemicals.

Growing lettuce in a garden

You can save water while brushing your teeth.

Some families talk about ways to take care of the environment on Earth Day. They may agree to turn off the water when they brush their teeth or to take shorter baths and showers. These steps save, or conserve (kuhn-SURV), water.

Family members might
remind each other to
recycle printer cartridges.
Old computers, cell
phones, and some batteries
can also be recycled.

Cell phones are electronic items that can be recycled.

A planter made from a milk carton

People talk about better ways to reuse items. Empty tissue boxes are good for storing many different things. Old milk jugs are perfect for watering plants. Paper gift bags and bows can be used again.

Can you think of some
things you can recycle
or reuse? Every day should
be Earth Day when it
comes to protecting
the environment.

Try to recycle or reuse something every day!

Words You Know

cell phones

chemicals

Gaylord Nelson

parade

pollution

recycle

tree

vegetable garden

31

Index

About the Author

Trudi Strain Trueit is a former television news reporter and weather forecaster. She has written more than thirty fiction and nonfiction books for children. Ms. Trueit lives near Seattle, Washington, with her husband Bill.

Photo Credits

Photographs © 2007: Corbis Images: 29, 31 top right (Peter Beck), cover (Jose Luis Pelaez, Inc.); Getty Images: 21, 31 bottom right (Tobi Corney/Stone), 6, 30 top right (Digital Vision), 25, 30 top left (Joe Raedle), 22 (Wide Group/Iconica); Index Stock Imagery/Shmuel Thaler: 14; Omni-Photo Communications/Barrie Fanton: 17; Photo Researchers, NY: 3 (Conor Caffrey), 5, 31 top left (Susan Leavines), 18, 31 bottom left (Will & Deni McIntyre); PhotoEdit/David Young-Wolff: 26; The Image Works/Lisa Law: 13, 30 bottom right; U.S. Senate Historical Office: 9, 30 bottom left.